Dealing With
DIVERSITY

The population of the United States is becoming increasingly diverse.

THE SCHOOL-TO-WORK LIBRARY

Dealing With
Diversity

Jeanne Strazzabosco

GLOBE FEARON EDUCATIONAL PUBLISHER
A Division of Simon & Schuster
Upper Saddle River, New Jersey

Published in 1996 by The Rosen Publishing Group, Inc.
29 East 21st Street, New York, NY 10010

First Edition

Printed in the United States of America

ISBN 0-835-91793-2

Contents

Many immigrants choose to maintain aspects of their native cultures. In New York's Chinatown, immigrants can buy Chinese foods and products and speak the language of their native land.

The Changing Face of America

BY THE YEAR 2000, ONLY 15 PERCENT OF NEW workers entering the workplace will be white males. The remaining 85 percent will consist of minorities and women. Currently, the population of the United States is approximately 260 million. Twelve percent of the population is African American, 7 percent Hispanic, 2 percent Asian, 1 percent Native American, and the remaining 80 percent Anglo (people of European origin). Whether in school or at work, you will find yourself working around classmates, co-workers, teachers, or supervisors of different backgrounds. It will be beneficial to understand this diversity. Your ability to recognize, understand, and be sensitive to diversity will help you to attain a high level of performance in school, the workplace, and eventually your career.

What exactly is meant by diversity? Among people, diversity simply means difference, whether in gender, race, age, culture, ethnicity, or physical ability. Every individual bears a unique set of characteristics that make him or her worthwhile and valuable.

The United States is no stranger to diversity. Since its beginnings, the United States has been made up of peoples of very diverse backgrounds. The first European settlers in America encountered the culture of Native Americans. In the early part of the 17th century, Africans were involuntarily brought to America as slaves. By the late 1700s, many of the Southern states were heavily populated by blacks. In the early 1800s, there was a great wave of voluntary immigration to the United States. These immigrants came mainly from Great Britain, Ireland, Scandinavia, and Germany. At the turn of the 20th century, a second wave of immigrants landed, mostly from southern and eastern Europe. The latest wave of immigrants began to arrive in the late 1960s, primarily from Asia and Latin America.

Each day our world becomes more diverse. In the 1990s, up to five million children of immigrant parents will be entering American public schools. Combined, these children will speak more than 150 languages other than English. One-fourth of the United States' twenty million foreign-born residents entered the country between 1985 and 1990. California is home to one-third of the foreign-born population. Other states with large concentrations are New York, Florida, Texas, New Jersey, and

Illinois. In a society that is becoming more diverse every year, it will be necessary to develop good interpersonal skills in order to be a productive, effective, and adaptable student and employee.

In the past, new immigrants learned to assimilate, or blend into the established American culture, to be accepted and to achieve success in their new country. This process of assimilation was compared to a melting pot. An unfortunate effect of the melting-pot approach was the loss of rich traditions, languages, and culture in favor of the established American culture. Today a new type of assimilation is beginning to evolve. Immigrants are no longer willing to abandon their language, customs, and traditions. They want to maintain aspects of their ethnicity and to speak and preserve their language. When looking at the population of the United States today, you no longer see a melting pot where cultures are blended until they all look the same. A mosaic is a much more accurate description of our society: A diverse yet positive representation of American people, each group adding a unique and useful element to the whole.

It's important to understand what is meant by culture. Everyone has a culture. It is made up of rules and expectations that are used when people interact. Culture is made up of an agreed upon set of rules for living that range from how to wear one's

Learning more about other cultures around the world can deepen your appreciation of diversity and help you avoid stereotypes.

hair to opinions about the creation of the world. Other aspects of culture are etiquette (how one behaves in various situations), values, language, traditions and customs, food, dress, and musical taste. Culture also includes belief systems and world views. Knowing about your own culture, and respecting the cultures of others, will prepare you for participation in today's multicultural world.

Stereotypes

When you don't know very much about a category of things, everything in that category looks similar. Take, for example, butterflies. A person who does not know much about them might picture them all like the Monarch butterfly, orange with a black border. Whenever the person thinks about butterflies, the image of the Monarch comes to mind. But once that person begins to study butterflies, he or she comes to realize how many kinds there are.

This happens with cultures as well. We pick up ideas about certain cultural groups from past experiences, rumor, or media influences and often assume them to be true for all group members. These ideas are called stereotypes or generalizations.

People use stereotypes to relieve anxiety. In a situation that isn't clear or when we experience behavior that is not predictable, we select a category in which to place another human being. We want to fit new information into our old files. This gives us a sense of control.

People misuse stereotypes when they don't think about their biases. Even positive stereotypes are dangerous because they limit our definition of a person. They are inflexible bits of information that do not apply to everyone. Stereotypical statements are applied to all members of a group without regard for individual differences. We should strive to eliminate stereotypes from our way of viewing others. The idea is to separate these generalizations from our genuine knowledge about cultural groups. The more we increase our knowledge about a group, the less likely we are to hang onto a stereotype.

Stereotypes are very often unreliable and untrue, and stem from perceived, not real, differences. Differences in skin color, physical ability, socioeconomic background, age, or gender may lead to stereotypes.

Paul Robeson, Jr., is an African American who studies American society and issues of diversity, prejudice, and discrimination. He tells a story in many of his lectures that beautifully shows how stereotypes and assumptions can play out in everyday life. On several occasions when he was booked to lecture at a major corporation, the limousine driver assigned to pick him up at the airport had trouble finding him because he had not been told to look for an African American. Robeson does not view this behavior as racial prejudice. The drivers were simply unable to think of an African American lecturing to white employees because of a stereotype they had acquired long ago.

Prejudice and Discrimination

Prejudice refers to a negative view or attitude about an entire group of people. It involves the prejudging of individuals based on their membership in a specific culture, race, ethnicity, or religion. It relies heavily on the use of stereotypes or generalizations about groups of people. Stereotypes are not necessarily harmful. They provide us with a starting place from which to expand our knowledge. Prejudice is the inappropriate use and exaggeration of stereotypes.

Discrimination is concerned with action and behavior. Discrimination refers to the treatment of individuals or groups differently because of prejudice. It means leaving someone out or punishing them because of prejudiced thinking. It is not based on knowledge of an individual's qualities, but on a label that marks that person inferior.

Prejudice and discrimination interconnect when

In our diverse society, it is important to eliminate prejudice and increase sensitivity toward diversity. Diversity can take many forms—age, gender, and ethnicity are just a few of the ways in which people differ.

individuals do not understand the history, experiences, values, and perceptions of ethnic groups that differ from their own. Lack of knowledge leads to stereotyping without thinking about differences within a group, and to judging other ethnic groups according to the standards and values of one's own group. It means thinking negatively about a particular group and seeing the qualities and experiences of other groups as less important than your own.

Prejudiced thinking brings about discrimination. It is unjust and destructive. This book will show you how to work toward eliminating prejudice and increasing sensitivity toward diversity.

Questions to Ask Yourself
The United States has always been characterized by diversity. In fact, our world becomes more and more diverse each day. 1) What does the term diversity mean? 2) What is a stereotype? What are some examples of stereotypes you have encountered? 3) How do prejudice and discrimination affect your life?

People often have different conceptions of personal space.

Key Elements of Cultural Identity

LANGUAGE PLAYS A SIGNIFICANT ROLE IN ETHNIC and cultural identification even after an ethnic group has joined another culture. Certain terms and phrases are held onto as a way to maintain and define group identity. Sometimes a cultural group does speak English, but its members may use words or language patterns such as Appalachian English, leading to cultural misunderstandings. Misunderstandings can be avoided once we recognize that all languages and all varieties of language are equally valid systems of communication and equally worthy of respect. Members of specific cultural groups should not be put down because of their speech. Think instead of the beauty of the new language patterns and the interesting new rhythms and sounds they offer.

Behaviors differ greatly from one cultural group to another. For example, each individual has a certain amount of personal space in which he or she feels most comfortable. Members of certain cultures prefer to stand a foot apart, whereas others are comfortable with three or more feet between them and others. Studies have shown that average Americans prefer eighteen inches to three feet, and Asians tend to allow at least three feet. Middle Eastern males and eastern and southern Mediterraneans maintain the least amount of personal space, zero to eighteen inches being the norm.

Another element of cultural identity is family. Cultures differ considerably as to what a typical family is and how that family behaves. Certain expectations and obligations to the family accompany each culture. Which relatives are considered close or distant is also a product of culture.

Gender roles are often determined in part by culture or background. Culture affects the ways in which males and females view their own gender. It affects their expectations for themselves as well as each other. Gender conflict and resolution styles also vary greatly among cultures.

Understanding Cultural Differences

Specific behaviors or norms connected with certain groups need to be recognized in order to avoid misunderstandings. For example, eye contact is a significant and meaningful behavior. Americans tend to think that people who avoid eye contact are uninterested, guilty, dishonest, or distracted. Other

An awareness of others' communication styles can improve your ability to understand and be understood.

cultures, however, play by different rules. Cambodian culture states that to look someone in the eye, particularly a superior, is to be rude and disrespectful. Members of certain European cultures make eye contact and maintain it much longer than Americans. All of these variances can be disconcerting without knowledge and understanding.

The use of pauses in conversation and silence vary from culture to culture. Some groups cannot tolerate long breaks in conversations and talk merely to fill the gaps; others look upon pauses as times of needed reflection. Remember that silence is not necessarily negative. In the workplace, make an effort, when appropriate, to match the communication style of your co-worker.

Americans generally value spontaneity as a sign of creativity and enthusiasm. In business, brainstorming sessions are often used to solve problems. Workers blurt out ideas at a rapid pace. Other cultures may view this behavior as rude and unwise. Some cultures choose to express themselves in a more careful manner, but it does not mean that they lack creativity or enthusiasm.

Volume of speech varies culturally, too. The rule in the United States is that an individual should speak neither too loudly nor too softly. Make an effort to match the other's tone when interacting.

A smile for Americans tends to be a sign of goodwill, a safe way to communicate friendliness and optimism. To other cultures, a smile can signal frivolity, inappropriate lightness. Don't give up smiling, but be aware that a smile does not carry a universal meaning.

Gestures can also cause misunderstandings. The American gestures for OK, like the "thumbs up," are among the most offensive to other cultures. Some have a strong sexual meaning. Calling to a person with your palm facing your body can be very demeaning; in certain cultures it is the way animals are called. Pointing is widely considered offensive and rude. It is not just who or what one points at, but the way in which one points. For example, consider the Asian and Middle Eastern avoidance of crossing the legs: when the legs are crossed, the bottom of the foot is showing and the toe could be pointing at someone. Even though you don't mean to be offensive, using a simple gesture could cause embarrassment for the other person.

A handshake is one of many ways in which we make an impression. Americans traditionally value a firm handshake. It is considered a sign of confidence and strength. Some individuals' handshakes are light in comparison. Handshakes do not reflect a personality, and we should take care not to project our own values and ideas onto others.

The meaning of touch also relates to a person's culture. You may be comfortable with a pat on the back or a squeeze of the shoulder, but not everyone feels that way. You risk offending and alienating a colleague. Cultures that place a high value on courtesy and formality and personal space also avoid touching. Cultures that need less personal space stand close to others when talking and tend to be more comfortable with touching. It is wise to avoid touching co-workers unless it is obviously appropriate; find other ways to communicate warmth and appreciation.

Some cultures place a high value on courtesy and formal behavior, particularly toward superiors. They

People may have different styles of communication.

may make a special effort to greet their superior every morning or decline a lunch invitation from a superior. Members of other culture groups do not feel comfortable speaking up at meetings. They may prefer to speak with co-workers or supervisors on a one-to-one basis. Many people feel uncomfortable talking about their accomplishments. They do not wish to appear boastful. A co-worker or manager who understands this might succeed in drawing them out so that workers with different backgrounds can be most effectively placed and adequately rewarded.

The value of being on time also differs among cultures. In the United States, being on time shows productivity and reliability. Being late to work, to an appointment, or with an assignment is to be lazy and uncaring. However, other cultures have a more leisurely style. Understand that lateness may be a culturally based behavior.

Questions to Ask Yourself

With the large number of different ethnic and cultural groups in our society, it is important to respect others' speech and behavioral identities. 1) How much personal space do you prefer to keep? How does that space differ from those of your friends? 2) What are some of the ways in which speech differs from culture to culture? 3) Why is it important not to touch co-workers? When would it be appropriate?

Diversity at School

3

TAKE A LOOK AT YOUR SCHOOL ENVIRONMENT. How many races, ethnic groups, and cultures are represented in the school's population? Is the population homogeneous (similar in background) or heterogeneous (with a variety of races, ethnicities, and cultures)? Go a step further and look at your own group of friends. Are they from diverse or similar backgrounds? Do you have equal numbers of male and female friends? If you and many of your friends are of the same race, ethnicity, or culture, look for opportunities to widen your scope of friendships. You may be comfortable with associating with people of similar cultures, but you can learn a lot from getting to know people who are different from yourself. When you take the time to get to know someone of a different background, you learn about a brand-new culture while at the same time sharing part of your own. It gives you the chance to compare and contrast. You'll think about issues you've never given thought to or noticed before.

Being comfortable with people of backgrounds different from your own will help you to be more comfortable with all kinds of diversity.

Learning About Diversity

There are many ways to increase your knowledge about diversity. Begin by exploring your own family history and roots. Find out where your ancestors came from. Have members of your family ever had to deal with discrimination or prejudice? Talk with older relatives about your heritage. Their knowledge and insight will be very valuable to you as you begin to learn more about your own background.

Many schools and college campuses have clubs that celebrate diversity. One western New York high school has a student organization called AACE, an acronym that originally stood for African American Cultural Excellence. The main focus of the group was to share African American history and culture with the student population. Unfortunately, students of other races and cultures did not accept the club. Many felt that the club was strictly for African Americans. The club's members realized the problem and decided to change their name—to All About Cultural Excellence. They also changed their goal to educating the school community about the diverse cultures their school represents and the unique contributions each group provides. Their membership now includes many races and cultures, including African Americans, Asians, Hispanics, Pakistanis, and whites. They sponsor assemblies at which members of the community speak about the

Communicating with students from other schools via e-mail or the Internet can help you learn about other ethnic, racial, or religious groups.

importance of recognizing and valuing cultural diversity. They hold informal discussions about the dangers of racism and sexism. They use role-playing activities to help the members better understand the perspectives of their friends and schoolmates. Perhaps your school already has such a group. If not, you could approach a teacher or administrator and discuss the benefits of beginning like a club AACE.

Choose a particular ethnic, racial, or religious group and learn as much as you can about them. Read local newspapers that are geared toward diverse cultural groups. Read books about different cultures. Visit and explore the community or part of town where students of different racial or ethnic backgrounds live? Have a meal in an ethnic restaurant or visit a local art gallery, museum, or theater. You will not only identify differences, but you will begin to understand and respect them.

Begin a student exchange with an urban/suburban school. Participating schools take turns visiting each other. They join in discussions about cultural awareness, as well as attend classes. Letter-writing and computer communication via e-mail or the Internet can take place among the students.

An alternative type of exchange that requires no transportation is distance learning. In distance learning, several sites work together through an interactive telecommunications network that helps them to communicate via fiber optic cable. The cable allows full audio and video interaction among sites. Students from different schools can talk to one another on television screens. Telecommunications networks are springing up everywhere. They publish programs of courses, workshops, and meetings, and can help you organize a distance learning event of your own.

A lot of information can be found right in your own newspaper. Pay attention to issues of cultural diversity when you read the news. Every day, there are stories about non-native speakers, racism, poverty, cultural traditions, gender, homosexuality, people with disabilities, and so on. Use the newspaper to find out what kinds of events are taking place that celebrate diversity. Maybe there is a foreign-language film or a film directed by a woman or a minority member that you can see. Cultural festivals take place all year long, especially in large cities. Make a real effort to experience something that is outside your area of expertise and comfort.

Studying a foreign language is another way to increase your knowledge of cultural diversity. While learning to communicate in the language, you will also discover the richness of the various races and cultures connected to it. High schools offer foreign languages as part of their regular list of electives, or you may find a community college in your area that

Check your local newspaper for information about foreign affairs.

offers a course in another language. It is not necessary to leave the United States to communicate in a language other than English. You can find opportunities right in your own community to practice a new communication skill. Later, in the workplace or in your chosen career, you will have a valuable skill, the ability to communicate in a language other than English. Businesses and corporations throughout the United States recognize the importance of this skill. Language schools have higher enrollments than before. Berlitz, a language school that leads the field in teaching foreign languages, reports that enrollments rose 47 percent from 1987 to 1992. This happened because executives want to conduct business with the waves of new immigrants arriving in the United States.

Volunteering can also increase your knowledge of diversity. Some high schools require a form of community service in order to graduate. Volunteer at a senior center to get experience with age diversity. Join a community action program that is building a playground for inner-city children. Volunteer at an AIDS hospice to gain insights into the world of the terminally ill. Volunteer as a guide in a local museum or be a reader for the blind. The Special Olympics need hundreds of volunteers to make their events a success. The list of areas in which you can offer to volunteer is endless. A counselor in your school can give you some ideas, or check in the yellow pages of your phone book.

Discrimination in School

In schools, discrimination makes the problems experienced by members of minority groups, females, and others even worse. Inequality in the classroom can be subtle or obvious. It causes terrible problems. An example of discrimination is when a teacher calls more upon male students than females to answer questions. Discrimination also takes place when students refuse to work cooperatively with students of a different race or ethnicity. People experiencing discriminatory behavior may feel isolated, depressed, unconfident, inadequate, or aggressive. Their self-esteem is lowered. If you witness or experience discrimination, bring it to the attention of a parent, teacher, counselor, or school administrator.

Success in school is affected by one's learning style. Everyone has a way of learning that works best for them. Some of us learn by listening; others learn best from reading. Columns and graphs work for some, while others function better with color and images. Some students feel comfortable arguing a point with a teacher in class, while others may have been raised to believe that this is disrespectful. Culture can affect an individual's learning style, but that does not mean that members of a certain race or culture have a certain learning style. However, some students are more likely to benefit from some teaching styles than from others. For example, some Native Americans prefer cooperative learning situations instead of competition. It is important to be aware of such tendencies in different cultural groups. Many teachers have had training to recognize, and accommodate, different learning styles. If you feel that your teachers do not understand your learning needs, talk to a school counselor or adviser about the possibility of a school-wide presentation on the topic of learning styles. Take the time to reflect on your learning, notice when you do your best work, and talk with your teachers so that they can help you succeed in school.

Questions to Ask Yourself

Your school environment is probably made up of people from a variety of different ethnic and cultural backgrounds. It is vital to take the time to associate with cultures other than your own. 1) What are some of the ways in which you can learn about different cultures? 2) Where can you look for information about other cultures? 3) Are there any volunteer programs you could join that would teach you about other cultures?

Diversity at Work

A PART-TIME OR SUMMER JOB CAN BE AN opportunity to experience diversity. You'll probably be working with people of different ages and backgrounds. This can be interesting and challenging, and sometimes difficult.

Stephen has been working as a bank teller since he graduated from high school three years ago. He has received excellent evaluations every year and is hoping to be promoted to head teller some day. He has a good relationship with his immediate supervisor, Matthew. Matthew is married and has children Stephen's age. They chat easily about their various interests. However, whenever Stephen mentions that he's working towards becoming head teller, Matthew puts him off with a remark about Stephen's age, and that he should be more concerned with youthful things like buying a car or dating.

Although Stephen likes and respects his manager, he feels more and more that he is being treated like

Talk to your employer if you feel you have been discriminated against in any way.

a kid. He wants to be taken seriously. Stephen decides to speak with Matthew and makes an appointment with him to discuss his future with the bank. He explains that his desire to become head teller is serious. He chooses his words carefully, telling Matthew that he has enjoyed his three years with the bank and that he has learned a great deal. He explains that he is interested in taking on more responsibilities and feels ready and capable for them.

After listening to Stephen, Matthew agrees that it may be time for Stephen to take on more responsibilities, and they discuss ways in which Stephen may begin to expand his role at the bank.

Stephen sensed that his supervisor was not

thinking about his promotion because he was young. Instead of accepting that he might be too young to do the job, Stephen went to his supervisor and explained to him why he thought he deserved a promotion. He presented his case honestly, and his employer listened.

Sometimes, like Stephen, you may feel that you are being discriminated against. Other times, you may find that you have to confront your own biases and stereotypes. It's important to develop the skills you need to deal with discrimination and prejudice.

Interpersonal skills are very important for success in the workplace. Participating as a member of a team requires good listening skills and knowing how to respond to others' contributions. Teaching others is another key skill that involves helping, coaching, informing, and assessing. When you interact with customers to serve their needs, you need to know how to listen actively to understand their needs and avoid misunderstandings. You need to be able to communicate in a positive manner. You may be called upon to exercise leadership. Leadership relies heavily upon good communication skills. You must also be skillful at negotiating to arrive at a decision. High performance in the workplace requires working effectively with cultural diversity. This means understanding one's own culture and the cultures of others, respecting the rights of others, making judgments and decisions based on performance, and understanding the concerns of other ethnic and gender groups. A worker who lacks an awareness of these things risks limiting his or her overall effectiveness.

In today's workplace, you need to be aware of and learn from the background or culture of your co-workers in order to communicate and work effectively. Culture is seen as a pattern of knowledge, skills, behaviors, attitudes, and beliefs held by a particular group and handed down from one generation to the next. Over the generations, it changes and evolves. A lot of energy and creativity can result from a diverse workforce. Employers are required by law to maintain a workplace that is free from any kind of discrimination on the basis of age, gender, race, national origin, or ethnic background. It is important to work hard to make sure that diversity is respected at your workplace. The unique contributions of all workers should be valued and respected.

Prejudiced remarks or inappropriate jokes should not be tolerated. It is everyone's responsibility to stop such behavior. If a co-worker refers to someone in an offensive or rude way, or generalizes about a specific group, it is important to speak up. Let the person know that you are not comfortable with stereotypes that put down other people. Using appropriate behavior yourself and being eager to learn

Inappropriate jokes that target specific groups should never be told among co-workers.

about new cultures help to counteract and eliminate prejudiced thinking.

When getting to know a co-worker, inquire about his or her family history instead of relying upon stereotypes for your questions. Do not assume, for example, that a co-worker did not grow up in the United States just because he or she is of a different ethnicity than you.

If you believe you are the victim of discrimination, you should inform a superior. If the behavior does not stop, you may wish to talk with an agency such as a local chapter of the Anti-Defamation League or the Equal Employment Opportunity Commission. Be aware of the possibility that your fellow co-workers may be taken advantage of, particularly if they come from disadvantaged groups. Is an employee who is learning English never given the change to work with customers, even though he or she is very friendly or capable? Be careful about making your own assumptions about co-workers' abilities based on factors they cannot control, such as disabilities, accents, age, or gender.

Watch Your Language!

Think about the language you use to be sure it is gender-neutral and free of all bias. Use expressions such as chairperson instead of chairman. Women make up a large percentage of today's workplace

Be sensitive to the difficulties of people for whom English is not a first language.

and should not be left out through the use of male-oriented language. Assumptions made based on gender are inaccurate, demeaning, and offensive.

You can use guidelines for communicating without racial and ethnic bias. Begin by being aware of words, images, and situations that give the impression that all or most members of a racial, ethnic, or gender group are the same.

Avoid qualifiers that support stereotypes. A qualifier is an added piece of information that suggests an exception to the rule. From the statement, "That black man is really intelligent," one could assume that the speaker believes that most blacks are not intelligent. "The woman doctor told me to rest for three days," implies that all doctors are male unless otherwise specified.

Identify people by race or ethnic origin only when relevant. The manager is an efficient leader, not an efficient Japanese leader. Few situations really require such identification.

Be aware of language that, to some people, has questionable racial or ethnic meanings. A word or phrase that may not be personally offensive to you may be so to others. "Culturally deprived" or "culturally disadvantaged" are terms that imply superiority of one culture over another. The term "reverse prejudice" also implies that a certain race or culture is always the target of prejudice.

Be Sensitive to New English Speakers

If you have ever traveled to a foreign country and tried to communicate in its language, you have probably felt the frustration, fear, and sense of inadequacy experienced by immigrants living in the United States. Many American-born workers were raised speaking a language other than English. Very capable, intelligent people who are learning a new language or even using a language that they've studied for years may seem inexperienced or difficult to understand. Avoid making assumptions and being misled about a person's ability based on their accent or level of English. There are ways you can help to lessen their feelings of frustration and inadequacy. Try to eliminate slang from your language if it might be misinterpreted. Instead of telling a non-native speaker of English that you're "taking off early from work," say that you're leaving work early. Examine your language to make sure it is clear and easy to understand. Let the non-native speaker finish what he or she is saying. The best way for a person to improve language skills is to practice. Invite a person who is learning English to have lunch with you and converse about more informal topics such as family and interests. This is a great opportunity to practice language skills in a way that is not so frightening.

Misunderstandings can happen because of generation gaps or generational differences among workers. The fact that you are different ages means that you have very different perspectives. Assumptions should not be made because of an individual's age. Also remember that everyone needs feedback and recognition. Try to understand each other's point of view. Take a close look at the person's background and make an effort to see his or her perspective.

Marie works as an engineer in a large corporation. She has been with the company since she graduated from college two years ago. Many of her co-workers are male, and Marie has established and maintained a positive relationship with them. It is important to have a solid relationship with her co-workers because much of her time is spent as part of a team, doing problem-solving. Being part of a team, Marie feels like an equal and respected contributor.

Once in a while, however, one of the engineers, Jeff, makes remarks or tells jokes that are offensive and rude to women. When she first heard Jeff making these remarks, she showed her disapproval by walking away. Later, Jeff told her that he wasn't talking about her, that she was different.

Unfortunately, Jeff's remarks and offensive jokes did not stop, and Marie decided that she could no longer tolerate the way they made her feel. She decided to talk with him, one-to-one. Marie explained how his jokes showed women as inferior to men, and that although he was trying to be funny his remarks were offensive and demeaning. She asked him how he would feel if she made similar remarks about all men being inferior. Jeff apologized and appreciated what Marie had to say. He promised to pay close attention to his remarks in the future.

Questions to Ask Yourself

Individuals of different ages and backgrounds must often learn to work together on the job. This can be a great opportunity to get to know someone from a culture other than your own. 1) What are some interpersonal skills that will help you to communicate effectively at work? 2) What kinds of behavior should you avoid displaying at work? 3) How can you make communication easier with people for whom English is a second language?

Diversity and Your Career

TODAY MORE THAN EVER, CORPORATIONS recognize the value of diversity. They see it as a positive thing and a way to achieve high economic performance. Corporations want to attract the best employees. With the labor force becoming more diverse, a company interested in long-term success must keep the best and the brightest employees from all backgrounds.

The rapidly changing demographics of the United States have created a new situation in which a diverse workforce is seen as a source of higher success and more creativity. From 1983 to 1993, the percentage of white male professionals and managers in the workforce dropped from 55 percent to 47 percent, while white women rose from 37 percent to 42 percent. The U.S. Labor Department estimates that by the year 2005 half of all new workers will be women, and more than one-third will be Hispanics, African Americans, and other minorities. Corporations also realize that they are

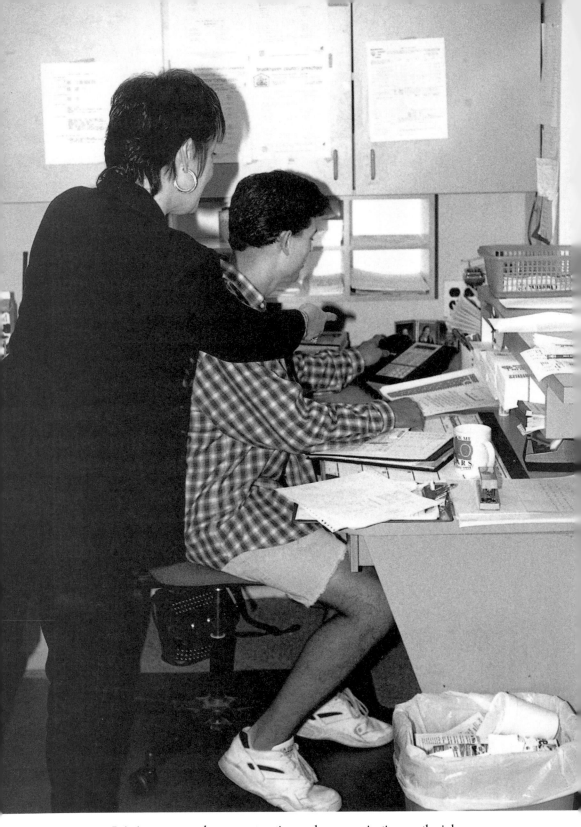

It is important to learn cooperation and communication on the job.

serving a much more diverse group of customers. If they fail to embrace diversity, they not only continue past injustices but also risk making their companies less successful.

This same realization is also taking place in Europe's new single market. European companies now desire "Euromanagers" who can work cooperatively and effectively with people from any country.

A professor at the University of North Texas performed an experiment in 1993 to find out if teams of people from different backgrounds could be more innovative and productive than teams that were similar in background. He studied the behavior of 173 students enrolled in a business-management course at a large university in the Southwest. The participants were divided into thirty-six teams of four or five. Seventeen teams were culturally homogeneous, all white, and nineteen were culturally diverse. The teams met on four occasions to analyze four different case-studies and to give solutions to the problems posed in these studies.

In the first two meetings, the homogenous groups did better than the diverse teams, but in the last two meetings the teams were equal. The culturally diverse teams found it more difficult to work together until their final meeting, when their ability to cooperate was just as good as that of the homogeneous teams. By the end of the experiment, the

Diverse groups of people can be more creative in accomplishing tasks.

diverse teams were clearly more creative than the homogeneous teams: They were able to examine the problems from wider perspectives and try more possible solutions in solving the final case study. The professor believed that if the experiment had continued for a longer period, the diverse teams would eventually have done better than the homogeneous teams. The conclusion from the experiment was that for companies to benefit from diversity, their workers need time and training to get past their differences and move toward productive cooperation.

The electronics industry has a solid base established in the Silicon Valley of California. Twenty years ago, when the industry was just beginning to take off, the workforce was made up of mostly white male engineers born in the United States. Today, the workforce is very diverse. The business community is now multicultural as a result of the immigration of professionals and other employees, mainly from Southeast Asia, India, and Mexico. With this diversity, there is a need for companies like Lingua-Tec, Inc. Lingua-Tec was founded in the early 1980s to help Silicon Valley companies improve cross-cultural communication. Many companies in the Silicon Valley needed help dealing with their new diversity.

One Silicon Valley company that surveyed the

Seminars and workshops can be organized to discuss issues of cultural sensitivity.

backgrounds of its 3,200 employees discovered thirty different nationalities that spoke forty languages and dialects. The company decided to institute a cultural awareness program because of the misunderstandings and tension between employees. One of the first programs taught employees to be more open in expressing their opinions. Communication and patience are stressed in the program. When listening to co-workers, it is important to consider their words along with their unique cultural backgrounds. To make sure you've understood co-workers, repeat or summarize what you've heard. Through this educational process, the company's employees not only raised productivity but also learned to value the ideas of people different from themselves.

Eastman Kodak Company has a goal to build, within ten years, a management team that reflects the diversity of the global markets it serves. The company's chief executive officer, George M.C. Fisher, has led an effort to redefine Kodak's mission, direction, and values. At Kodak, they've recognized a need to increase the diversity of their professional and management ranks to include more women and minorities. Kodak's mission statement states, ". . . we want to deliver total customer satisfaction through a diverse team of energetic employees with world-class talent and skills necessary to sustain Kodak as the world leader in imaging."

In 1995, the U.S. Department of Labor selected Xerox Corporation as the first recipient of the Glass Ceiling Award, a tribute to the company's thirty-year effort to hire and promote minorities and women in key jobs, known as the balanced workforce approach. The glass ceiling refers to invisible barriers that still block women and minorities from executive positions. According to the company's CEO, Paul A. Allaire, diversity in their workforce is more than a necessity. It is a business opportunity. The balanced workforce approach has allowed Xerox to set goals and measure whether or not they are eliminating inequalities and imbalances. Presently, 18 percent of Xerox senior managers are members of minority groups. Approximately 20 percent are women, and 24 percent of the corporate offices are held by women or minorities. By the end of 1994, the Xerox document-processing workforce in the United States was 14 percent black, 7 percent Hispanic, 5 percent Asian and 1 percent Native American. Women represented 32 percent of the entire workforce.

Today's high performance economy needs employees who can work well with men and women from a variety of ethnic, social, or educational backgrounds. A successful worker will depend heavily on interpersonal skills. He or she must be aware of and sensitive to body language, cross-cultural communication, gender-neutral language, and gender-related differences in the workplace.

Many U.S. companies and corporations have started cultural awareness programs and seminars. Some have actually appointed new directors in charge of staffing and diversity. When you're ready to begin to interview with companies, do some research to see how the companies manage and promote diversity. Do they have diversity training for their employees? Find out their philosophy toward workforce diversity and compare it to the numbers of diverse workers employed. Also look for

A successful worker in today's economy must be aware of and sensitive to body language
and cross-cultural communication.

information about the number of minorities and women holding upper-level positions.

The Anti-Defamation League will come to an office and conduct their seminar called "A World of Difference." The goal of the Anti-Defamation League is to eliminate prejudice while promoting the acceptance and celebration of diversity. Co-workers come together to take part in large and small group discussions. The facilitators guide the groups through topics that deal with prejudice and discrimination. Upon completion, the participants are better able to recognize and confront prejudice in themselves and others.

Some companies have video libraries for their employees that deal with diversity in the workplace. The videos contain meaningful dialogues among people of different backgrounds. They discuss issues of diversity in a frank and open manner that is help-ful to a person seeking to increase his or her knowl-edge of different races and cultures.

In these videos, members of various groups ex-plain that they want to be seen as individuals with names, not as members of a group. For this reason, be sensitive to using labels. Approach a person tact-fully and respectfully when asking what their ethnicity is. They may be pleased at your curiosity, as long as it is expressed appropriately.

It is important to move past harmful stereotypes,

Tasting the foods of different cultures can be a fun way to broaden your horizons.

such as the beliefs that all Native Americans live on reservations, Hispanics are slow learners, or all Italian Americans are involved in organized crime. Many Native Americans live in cities and suburbs. English is not the first language for some Hispanics, but that does not mean that they are slow learners. Very few Italian Americans have dealings with organized crime. Physically disabled people feel the hurt of being stereotyped when employers or co-workers assume that they are not able to perform their jobs effectively. People with disabilities also notice when co-workers have trouble looking them in the eye. All people want others to take the time to get to

People with disabilities are entitled to the opportunity to excel in the workplace and should never be judged on the basis of a physical disability.

know them and find out what they're like. They are unique individuals who have different interests and abilities.

Discrimination can be very subtle. Laws and regulations have made it illegal to practice open discrimination, but sometimes people can show their biases in other ways. A boss who chats more easily with workers of his or her own ethnicity, or who assigns slightly more important tasks to men than to women, may not be breaking the law but is definitely treating people unfairly. Be aware of your own behavior and feelings toward others. Do you feel more comfortable with people just like you? Do you have assumptions such as "Older people are slow" or "Anyone younger than me doesn't know as much as I do"? It is human nature to buy into stereotypes and make assumptions. Recognize stereotypes and assumptions in your own thinking, and try to break free of them. Life will be much more interesting when you consider each person as an individual, not as a member of a group.

If you hold a supervisory position someday, you will need to be especially aware of how you treat others. There will be times when you need to address employees' performance and behavior. Communication and sensitivity are your best tools in these types of situations. Respect the rights of the employees under your supervision by making judgments based on performance, not stereotypes. Try to understand any special concerns employees may have.

You've probably heard the old saying, "Treat others as you want to be treated." This is a good thing to keep in mind when thinking about issues of diversity. Just as you might consider others different from yourself, they probably have their own reasons for thinking that you are different. Yet these things that make you different are the same things that make you unique. Nobody else has the same combination of personality and experiences that you have. Thinking about difference in this positive way may help you to approach others with a more positive attitude. Every time you meet someone with values and opinions that differ from your own, you enrich your own perspective.

When dealing with diversity, the main goal is to communicate respect for the worker's culture. Acknowledge that differences exist among peoples and cultures, and make a commitment to expose yourself to people from diverse groups and learn about their diversity. Face the fact that your own culture has not cornered the market on the truth. We can learn from other cultures and along the way realize that our way may not be the only way. Remember that multicultural education is a process. It is ongoing, constantly changing, and dynamic.

Have enough confidence in your own values and culture so that you do not feel intimidated by diversity. You can still be yourself while communicating respect for the diverse values and cultures of others.

Questions to Ask Yourself

Today's corporations are on the lookout for bright employees from diverse backgrounds. Understanding diversity and other cultures is an important quality to have in achieving your career goals.
1) What are the benefits to having a culturally diverse workplace? 2) Which large companies are

recognized for their diverse workplaces? 3) How can you apply your knowledge of diversity to achieve your career goals?

Glossary

alienate To become unfriendly or indifferent.

culture The totality of socially transmitted behavior patterns, arts, beliefs, institutions, and all other products of human work and thought, characteristic of a community or population.

curriculum All the courses of study offered by an educational institution.

demographics The statistical features of a population, such as age, income, race, or ethnicity.

dialect Regional variety of a language distinguished by pronunciation, grammar, or vocabulary. A variety of speech differing from the standard literary language or speech pattern of the culture in which it exists.

discrimination The act of making distinctions; to act on the basis of prejudice.

diversity The fact or quality of being diverse, different.

ethnic Of or pertaining to a religious, racial, national, or cultural group.

immigrant One who leaves a country to settle permanently in another.

minority Racial, religious, political, national, or other group regarded as different from the larger group of which it is a part.

negotiate To confer with another in order to come to terms or reach agreement.

prejudice An adverse judgment or opinion formed beforehand or without knowledge or examination of the facts.

punctual Acting or arriving exactly at the appointed time; prompt.

racism The notion that one's own ethnicity is superior.

sexism Discrimination based on sex. Attitudes or conditions that promote stereotyping of social roles based on gender.

stereotype A person, group, event, or issue considered to typify or conform to an unvarying pattern or manner, lacking any individuality.

For Further Reading

Anti-Defamation League. *A World of Difference.* Albany NY: Anti-Defamation League, 1986.

Coedeiro, Paula; Reagan, Timothy; and Martinez, Linda. *Multiculturalism and Total Quality Management—Addressing Cultural Diversity in Schools.* Newbury Park, CA: Corwin Press, 1994.

Johnson, Otts. *Information Please.* Boston & New York: Houghton Mifflin Company, 1994.

Robeson, Paul, Jr. *Paul Robeson Speaks to America.* New Brunswick, NJ: Rutgers University Press, 1993.

Thiederman, Sondra. *Bridging Cultural Barriers for Corporate Success.* Lexington, MA: D.C. Heath, 1991.

U.S. Department of Labor, The Secretary's Commission on Achieving Necessary Skills. *Learning a Living: A Blueprint for High Performance.* Washington, D.C.: U.S. Government Printing Office, 1992.

Index

About the Author
Jeanne Strazzabosco is a free-lance writer and translator. She works full time as a teacher of French and Spanish at a junior high school in Rochester, New York.

Photos
Cover, © B. Martin/The Image Bank. P. 6, © Patti McConville, The Image Bank; p. 14, AP/Wide World. All other photos by Matthew Baumann and Kim Sonsky.

Layout and Design
Kim Sonsky